SECURING YOUR HOME

A GUIDE TO INEXPENSIVE HOME SECURITY

ISBN# 978-0-6152-2379-7

Securing Your Home

CONTENTS

INTRODUCTION

A home truly is a person's castle. The safety found within the walls of your home is priceless. As homeowners, renters, and residents you cherish the place where you live. This is a place where you secure your possessions, raise your children, and lie down each night to sleep.

Across the world, millions of homeowners and renters fall victim to home invasion. Likewise, small and large businesses become subject to illegal entry, vandalism and theft. Often times, home owners live in fear, wondering if they will be the next victim of home invasion. These fears are real and should not be taken lightly. More so than ever before, criminals choose homes simply by random chance- they drive down any given road, pick a house and break inside. Nobody in today's society can honestly say that they are not a possible target for a home invasion.

In this book you will learn simple techniques that will help you to secure your home. These cost effective methods will help you to get the most of your dollar and still provide adequate security for your home, apartment, property and family. On a personal note, when I first began working on the security of my own home I had little cash to invest in a system. Money can get tight and a large investment into security was not an option. However, after careful planning and study I was able to create a cost effective system that involved analyzing my home and determining what I could do to prevent an unwanted intrusion. The ideas within this book can help you too in securing your home without going broke in the process.

OUTLOOK &

DEVICES

Chapter 1

OUTLOOK

The outlook on crime in the near future can be somewhat discouraging as the crime rate tends to increase in most cities. Depending on where you live, the rate of crime will vary. For example, New York City will have a much higher rate of crime than Jackson Hole, Wyoming. Nonetheless, crime happens everywhere, in every city- almost everyday. And history has shown time and again that many of the most dangerous or hostile crimes happen in rural communities rather than large cities.

When speaking of home invasion the common intruder can be broken down into two categories, those who intentionally invade specific target locations and those who just choose randomly. Both types can be very dangerous and should not be taken lightly. The strategies and techniques explained in this book will help to deter both types of criminals.

Home intruders who plan their targets attempt to learn the lay of the land and the habits of the residents. They will case a home, property or business and observe the daily activities of those who reside there or frequently visit. They take careful note as to when the location is vacant of any people and how long they are absent. They also observe the neighbors, mailman and any other delivery personnel that my come by.

As the potential intruder begins to figure out the patterns of every resident and learns the most vulnerable times for the home, he will then work on learning the set up of and the weak spots in the security. This research may include casually walking up to the front door and checking the door knob to see if it is locked. If the opportunity presents itself, other doors and windows will be checked as well. Often times, he will find a door or window left unlocked but will not make his intrusion right then. However, he now know's a weak spot to the location and will make that a potential entry when committing the crime.

Security systems are often a hang up for home intruders unless they are first aware of what they are dealing with. There are many security companies who proudly post their signs in the front yards of their customers to help deter would be thieves. While this tactic may work to fend off petty thieves, it may have the opposite effect on a professional burglar. Instead of scaring away the intruder, these little signs help inform the criminal of what he will encounter when breaking and entering. Some security companies place their security control panels in specific or predictable locations throughout the house or

6

business. With basic knowledge of the various security companies and how they operate, an intruder can factor in the disabling of the security system during the invasion process.

Intruders who spend a significant amount of time casing a specific target know what they are after. They have chosen that home, or apartment because of something in particular that they can only get there. This can range anywhere from money to family possessions and even children or potential rape victims. Premeditated crimes are often successful when given enough preparation, but it is also possible to prevent such events from occurring. Other premeditated intrusions are often performed by people that you know, even family. They already know the set up of the location and therefore can successful break in without little restraint. Trust becomes your best defense in these types of situations and will be discussed later in this book.

Random intrusions are often times drug related. Illegal drugs such as crystal meth can have a powerful effect on the human brain, causing people to make drastic and disastrous decisions. One method of forced entry that has gained popularity over the years is when an intruder simply kicks in a door or window and rushes the home or business owner before they have a chance to react. Once inside, the intruder will either, bind, severely injure or even kill the owner before proceeding to commit the initial crime. Rape has often occurred as a result of this type of illegal entry. Often times an intruder will break through a door in search of drugs or cash and will find a vulnerable female resident. Instead of just taking the money and running he will push his luck and rape the victim before leaving the scene.

Random intruders can also include thoughtless teenagers who dare one another to sneak into a home after dark. Transients passing from town to town choose randomly when looking to invade a home or business.

Committing an illegal entry holds no set standards. Though some methods are used more than others, the only true relation between all the various types of illegal entries is the fact that they are crimes committed against another person. It is important to know how to combat any type of invasion that can or may occur to your home or property. NO SYSTEM IS BULLET PROOF!! But some methods of crime prevention are more effective than others. This book will further explain how to safeguard your residence without spending too much money.

SECURITY DEVICES

There are so many security devices out on the market today that it becomes difficult to determine which one is best for you. Depending on the type of security device and brand name, expenses may vary considerably. One of the biggest misconceptions in today's world is the mindset that the most expensive products are always the best. While this assumption may be true in many regards, it does not necessarily apply to the security industry.

Alarm Companies

As you drive through your town or neighborhood you may notice security signs in people's yards or windows. These signs indicate that the home or business is being protected by an alarm/alert system. Inside the home, sensors are placed strategically in various rooms and on doors and windows. These sensors are motion or sound activated and will sound off an alarm when an unplanned entry had occurred. Also, the alarm system will call the companies dispatchers indicating that there is an intruder and the dispatcher then notifies the local police. These alarms often include smoke detectors and even carbon monoxide alarms.

In theory, these types of systems should be more than adequate for home protection. However, not only are they expensive but they often fall short of success do to human error or misunderstandings.

EXAMPLE: In my own neighborhood I have witnessed one such home where, while the owners were on vacation, the alarm went off. The loud system could be heard by the neighbors next door. The neighbor, having a key to the residence and permission to enter the home if necessary, eventually went in to investigate. The neighbor knew about the system and that it was to notify the company of any danger or problems. After shutting off the alarm, the neighbor then called the company to ensure that all was well. Much to his surprise, the company knew nothing about the alarm and therefore had contacted no one. Somewhere along the way, the system was not communicating with the dispatcher or the dispatcher had simply failed to recognize the alert.

Not every alarm company should be branded for one company's mistakes. There are many alarm and alert companies who strive hard to satisfy their customers and provide adequate security and smoke detection. A positive example would be Peak Alarm located in Utah. Their employees must first pass a Federal Background check and then receive proper training by professional instructors.

The downside to these types of security companies is the cost, the billing and the hassle of installation. If the cost of one of these systems fits well into your financial situation then perhaps they are the best solution for securing your property. However, most home and business owners are hesitant when it comes to sinking large numbers into security. They know that it is important but difficult to justify, especially in a low crime area.

Door and Window Alarms

There is little doubt that the most vulnerable places on a home are the doors and windows. There have been exceptions to this rule such as intruders passing through a chimney or even crashing through a wall with a vehicle. Duplexes and apartments that share walls can be accessible by cutting through the wall from the neighboring side. To prevent this, additional security measures, mentioned later in this book, would have to take place.

Doors and windows are the easiest methods of entering a building, especially when the intruder wishes to go undetected or wants the element of surprise. Most alarm systems focus on these vulnerable spots by using magnetic alarm systems and motion sensors. Other alarms for protecting windows include sensors that beep when the glass vibrates in any way.

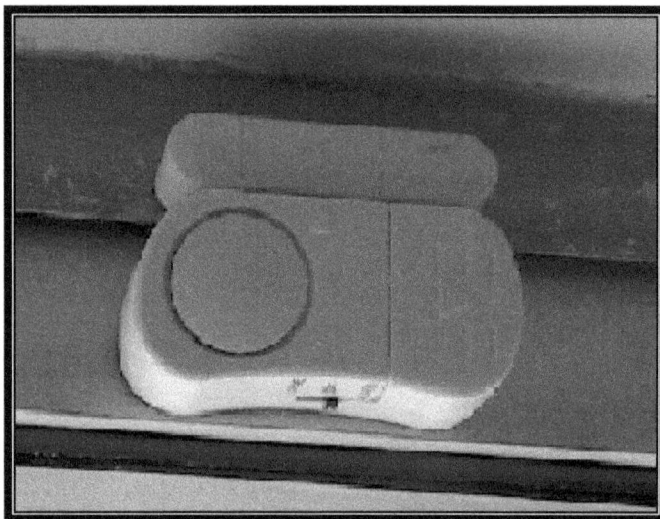
Magnetic Alarm

Magnetic Door/ Window Alarms are an inexpensive and highly effective way for securing doors and windows. Their purpose is not to prevent an illegal entry but rather alert home owners when one is occurring. Though the intentions of this type of alarm is not to keep someone out such as a lock would do, the loud alarm will often scare a intruder and cause them to flee the scene.

Magnetic alarms have two basic parts- the wall mount and the door or window mount. On each part there is a magnetic or metallic strip that would face together when the door or window is closed. On one of the two parts there is a button or switch which can be moved to turn on the alarm or disable it. When the switch is set to the alarm and the strips are faced together, the alarm will not go off. When the switch is set on the alarm and the door or window is moved causing the strips to separate, the magnetic break will cause the alarm to sound. Most of these devices, though small, can be heard throughout an entire home or building. Only by realigning the strips or flipping the switch to off will the alarm cease to sound.

Some of the advantages to magnetic alarms are their simple, yet effective design. They are light weight, easy to use, install and are loud enough to panic any intruder. Furthermore, these alarms are relatively inexpensive, costing between $4.00 to $50.00 depending on brand and model. Battery operated alarms are generally less expensive and more dependable as long as the batteries are changed periodically. Electronic alarms that depend on a power source can be rendered useless during a power outage or if the power is shut off intentionally by an intruder.

<u>Door Locks</u>

Most homes are equipped with locking doors and windows. The lock for a door may be assembled right into the door knob or handle. These types of cylinder locks are effective in keeping out many unwanted intruders but the system is never bullet proof. Lock picking has become more popular over the years and access to the right tools is merely a click away on the internet. With a little practice using a basic lock pick set, door locks can easily be mastered. The basic design of this lock consists of the cylinder which the key is pressed into. Inside are a series of 5 or more different length pins that release the cylinder into motion when the key lines them up. The teeth on a key balance out or compensate for the different sizes of pins and when pressed together, create an even surface on the top of the pins.

If an intruder wishing to break into a home wants to enter by picking this type of lock, they would need a lock pick set which consists of different shaped picks and one or two tensioners. At this time I will not go into detail as to how to pick a lock with a lock pick set, but rather I will simply say that by putting tension on the cylinder and racking the pins, a person can line up the pins much like a key and therefore release the cylinder into motion.

Dead bolt locks are much the same in setup as your common door knob lock. Granted, newer designs may have several pins creating a more complicated pin combination, but the selling point to a dead bolt lock is the large latch that hooks the door to the door frame. Seeing that large bolt engage from the door into the wall gives homeowners a sense of security. In reality, this type of lock can be just as easy to pick as any other cylinder lock. Regardless of how strong the bolt may be, if the lock itself can be breeched then the bolt is useless.

Most of your common thieves will not know how to pick a lock. Many intruders who cannot afford a lock pick set or don't know how to use one, prefer to take a more bold approach at forced entry- they simply bust their way in. This type of entry can be done by breaking a window or even driving a vehicle through the front door. To prevent such an intrusion interior locks and latches may be needed.

Interior Locks and Latches

Though dead bolts can easily be picked much like a lock in a door knob, dead bolts do have their place in security. With the large bolt connecting the door and frame, an intruder is less likely to gain access by kicking or ramming the door open, providing the frame and door are well structured around the bolt.

Along these same lines there are other latch or bolt type locks that help to better secure a door from intruders who try to force the door open. You probably have seen several different types of interior locks, some of which have a chain that connects the door and frame. These locks are good in theory but lack the strength necessary to secure against a hard kick or slam against the door. Most of the link to these chains are weak and cannot withstand the pressure. Also, the glide in which the chain connects to the wall can also be ineffective in holding the chain under extreme pressure.

Another type of latch is a long, almost an oval shaped bar that overlaps a small metal arm on the door or wall. When the door is opened, the latch binds with the arm preventing the door from opening. Like the chain, it can only be unlocked with the door is fully closed. Though stronger than the chain lock, this too can only handle so much pressure before breaking.

The most basic type of interior lock is simply the straight latch which slides from the door into a metal hole or ring attached to the wall. Unlike the two locks previously mentioned, this type of latch will not allow you to partially open the door without unlocking it. However, in its simple design, this instrument can provide the most security for your door and even on some windows.

Two disadvantages to interior locks is first, the effectiveness of the lock all depends on the strength of your door and frame. And second, you cannot lock or unlock the latch device from the outside, leaving it useless during your absence.

Doors and Windows

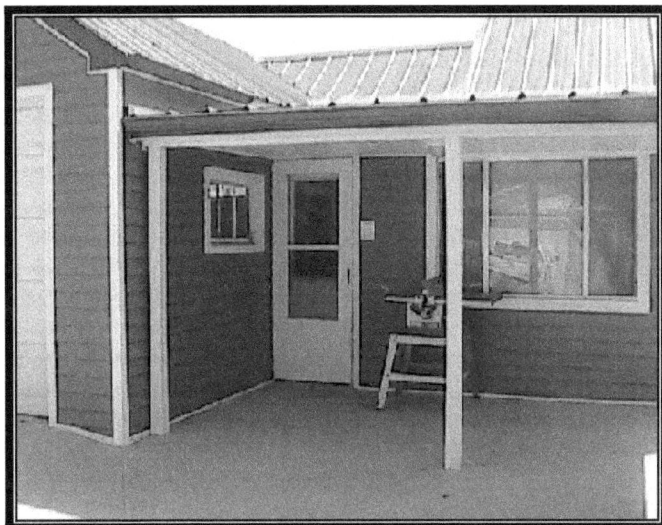

A sturdy door is the most important aspect of protecting the entry way into your home. A solid wood or metal door will provide superior protection against a forced or kicked entry. Because of the door's solid design, stronger locks can be installed on them which will maximize security. The frame around the door must also be strong and well designed to make the lock(s) effective. When examining your exterior doors, look from the outside and imagine the door being force or kicked in. What would be the primary breaking point?

On a weak or flimsy door, the wood around the knob or lock will break under pressure. Cheap framework will also break apart under a heavy kick. The bolt or latch from the door knob assembly and any other lock will act as a hammer busting through the wood. Strong doors prevent crime!

Windows are also susceptible to forced entry. Little can be done to secure glass unless you are willing to pay the expensive price for bullet/shatter proof glass. But windows have come a long way in design and can now hold up to a significant amount of pressure before breaking. Many windows will shatter but not break down into small pieces. An intruder would still have to break through the spider web glass.

The best defense for a window would be a vibrating alarm which can detect any cutting or extreme movement of the glass itself. This method may not keep an intruder out but it will give you a warning to a home invasion.

Lighting

Most intruders prefer to work under the cover of darkness. One way to prevent an invasion into your home is to make it less vulnerable from the outside. With a home well illuminated, thieves are often deterred and forced to look elsewhere for a break in.

Exterior lighting can be a great method of crime prevention, but it can also be an annoyance to neighbors and drivers who are passing by. For most homes of average size, incandescent or fluorescent type floodlights shining down along each side of a home, aiming to the ground will provide adequate exposure without bothering the neighbors. Lights can also be placed throughout the property to expose any possible cover for an intruder.

Interior lighting can also help to deter crime, especially in homes that have a lot of windows. Many fast food restaurants will leave the lighting on behind the counter after the business is closed. This will make an intruder visible for anybody passing by especially patrolling police officers who know what to look for.

The downside to interior and exterior lighting is its dependency on electricity. When the power source is cut off, the light will cease to work. An experienced burglar or intruder will cut or disconnect the power source, causing the lights to shut off prior to their invasion. Battery backup systems can help to prevent this as can lights that are dependent on solar power rather than electricity fed from the home. Solar lighting will also save on expense as prices of residential power continue to increase. To further save on expense and power, motion activated lighting will help to turn the lights on only when necessary. This feature adds to the security of a home because it alerts the homeowner when someone or something is moving about inside the perimeter of the yard.

Landscaping

Nothing is more painful than falling into a large cactus or thorn bush. Each prick from a needle or thorn can throb for days and even cause infection. It doesn't take a person long to figure out that these plants are better left untouched.

Plants such as thorn bushes and cactus can serve as an effect security device when placed under vulnerable windows. Even if the intruder wanted to remove or cover these plants to allow access to the window, thorn bushes are noisy when rustled and cacti hold firm to the ground with their roots. Simply pushing them aside is not an option.

Choosing the right plant for your yard depends heavily on where you live. Cold climates can be difficult for many cacti while other plants depend on shade and amount of moisture. For the best results, contact your local nursery and tell them of your intentions to have a thorn bush below your windows. Be prepared with information about where the plant will be located and how much sunlight and water it will receive.

Fences and Gates

Depending on the type of yard or structure you may have, a fence can add additional security to your establishment. If a business has a courtyard, parking lot or storage area a fence may be necessary to help regulate the flow of traffic and visitors. Much like any other security device, fences are not impassible; however, they will prevent the theft of large objects as well as deny access to anyone unwilling to scale the fence.

Chain link fences provide excellent security for both home and business. Though they are not as attractive looking as a wood or stone fence, the prices are competitive with other types of fences and require little maintenance. For home based businesses with a lot of outside storage it is recommended that barb or razor wire be strung on the top, angled outward to prevent intruders from climbing over the top.

A chain link fence should be made of at least 9 gauge wire. The U.S. Department of Defense recommends that it stand seven feet tall with a gap no higher than 2 inches at the bottom. When deciding to install a chain link fence, talk with a professional installer and explain why you want a fence and what it is you are protecting. An experienced installer should be able to tell you what you need and save you unnecessary expenses.

For most residential homes, a chain link fence in the back yard should be at least six feet tall. Having a chain link fence in the front can also add security, but many are turned off by its cold appearance. However, a 4 foot chain link fence can actually look attractive in a front yard as well as provide a small amount of security around the perimeter.

Animals

Many people enjoy the companionship of a loyal dog. Others simply keep dogs for security and perimeter controls such as in junk yards and fenced in facilities. Animals, mainly dogs, can be a great alarm, alert and protection system for homeowners and even certain types of businesses. However, keeping an animal requires a lot of attention. Dogs can be the most loyal friend a person will ever have. To abuse or neglect one is not only inhumane but also despicable, irresponsible and against the law. When a dog is treated kindly, loved and fed well, it will do everything to defend its master and territory, regardless of its size.

Before purchasing a dog, think about how it will affect your lifestyle and if your home and living conditions are animal friendly. Dogs need space to run, and much like a child, they need love and attention. If you are unable to provide these bare necessities then dog ownership is highly discouraged. Furthermore, you will also have the expense of food, veterinarian visits, and possibly grooming to pay for. If you frequently travel then care for the animal will have to be arranged during your absence. Too often, people will adopt a new pet without considering the many responsibilities that it will require.

If your home and living conditions meet the standards necessary to have a dog, big or small it will bring new excitement into your life and also serve as a warning device when someone is near your home. Not only do dogs have an incredible sense of smell but they can also hear the smallest sounds that would never register with human ears. They also have a keen sense of judgment and know when their loved ones are in danger or if an approaching stranger is a threat. If you have small children in the home a female dog will often be more protective of them and gentler than a male.

<u>Firearms</u>

Different from all the above mentioned devices and methods for crime prevention, firearms are rarely considered for home defense. When placed in the right hands, a firearm can serve as a positive weapon for personal defense. However, in terms of preventing trespassing or home invasion, firearms are not an option. Preventive security should never include serious bodily harm or death.

Home/business invasion preventive methods are created to keep out intruders, warn homeowners, and deter possible crimes from occurring. Firearms, though sometimes used to threaten home intruders, are not a preventive tool but rather a protection device. For example, suppose John Doe has an alarm system on his home. One night, an intruder breaks one of John's windows and climbs in. The alarm sounds and John is alerted. Upon hearing the alarm, the intruder panics and runs away. This is a preventive method of security.

Now let's suppose that instead of running away, the intruder pulls out a knife and charges for John Doe in an attempt to commit bodily harm. John pulls a pistol and fires, killing the intruder. This action would be considered self defense.

Owning a firearm requires great responsibility and training. Guns are at their most dangerous when they are resting in untrained hands. If you desire to become a gun owner for personal protection, please contact a licensed instructor for training. The National Rifle Association (NRA) is a great source for firearm information and training. They, along with licensed Concealed Weapons Permit Instructors, shooting instructors and firearm manufacturers can all provide information on how and when to use a firearm, as well as how to safely store one. When it comes to owning a gun, remember SAFETY FIRST!

CONDUCTING A RISK ASSESSMENT SURVEY

Chapter 2

RISK ASSESSMENT
Chapter 2

Conducting a Risk Assessment (RA) is the first step in securing your home. By following an RA outline, you will ensure that all areas of weakness have been found. An RA will also help save you money as you figure out how much security your home or property really needs.

Here is a basic outline for conducting a risk assessment for a residential location. This outline also includes the property that surrounds the home.

RISK ASSESSMENT SURVEY

1. Personal Information

Name:

Address:

Number of occupants:

Occupations:

Animals / Types:

Amount of Time Present:

Hours unoccupied:

2. Perimeter

Roads connected to property (how, how many):

Amount of traffic:

Location within city / neighborhood:

Perimeter entrances/ how many, accessibility:

ENTRANCE	LOCKS	NECESSITY	ACCESSIBLE	CONCERN

Condition of yard:

Fence / type / condition:

FENCE TYPE	CONDITION	PLACES/ NEED OF IMPROVEMENT

Gates / locks / who has access:

LOCATION	LOCKS	NECESSITY	ACCESSIBLE/WHO?	CONCERN

Neighbors (Who, how many, problems, level of trust, history, interaction):

NAMES (10 AND UP)	*TRUST	HISTORY, INTERACTION, CONCERNS

*Level of Trust – 1-10 One being extremely untrustworthy, ten begin fully trustworthy

Garage/ shed (Condition):

Contents within outside structure (flammable liquids, tools, ATV):

OBJECT	VALUE	ACKNOWLEDGED, (WHO KNOWS)

Exterior lighting (YES OR NO):
A.   Is the yard completely illuminated?
B.   Is the exterior walls of the home completely illuminated?
C.   Are the lights in full operation?
D.   Are the lights easily accessible?
E.   Are the lights easy to operate?
F.   Are the lights controlled from inside?
G.   Is there a battery backup for these lights?

If you have answered NO to any of these questions, please explain:

Motion sensors / security system:

A.   Type and brand of sensor/ alarm:

B.   Objective of the sensor/alarm (what does it do /cover?):

C.   How does it operate?

D.   Performance history:

Mail box (condition, type, locking, vandalized):

Vehicles/ amount / movement:

TYPE	CONDITION	VALUE	MOVEMENT

Have you ever caught someone in your yard before who did not have permission?

3. Exterior of home

Color:

General shape / design of home:

Wall and structure material:

Condition:

Windows (Exterior and Interior inspection)
 * Height from the ground

LOCATION	CONDITION	LOCK/ ALARM	HEIGHT*	EXPOSURE

Height and condition of roof (Are there any low accessible places?):

Entry Ways & Doors

ENTRY WAY #1
    A.   Is the entry way or porch clean?
    B.   Is the entire entry visible from inside the home?
    C.   Is the entry way well lit?
    D.   Does the entry way have steps?
    E.   Are there additional doors besides the door to the house?
    F.   Is the entry way enclosed? If so, can it be locked?

Door
    1.   Condition:

    2.   Strength:

    3.   Usage:

    4.   Locks:

    5.   Peep hole or alarm:

ENTRY WAY #2
    A.   Is the entry way or porch clean?
    B.   Is the entire entry way visible from inside the home?
    C.   Is the entry way well lit?
    D.   Does the entry way have steps?
    E.   Are there additional doors besides the door to the house?
    F.   Is the entry way enclosed? If so, can it be locked?

Door
    1.   Condition:

    2.   Strength:

    3.   Usage:

    4.   Locks:

    5.   Peep hole or alarm:

ENTRY WAY #3

A. Is the entry way or porch clean?
B. Is the entire entry way visible from inside the home?
C. Is the entry way well lit?
D. Does the entry way have steps?
E. Are there additional doors besides the door to the house?
F. Is the entry way enclosed? If so, can it be locked?

<u>Door</u>

1. Condition:

2. Strength:

3. Usage:

4. Locks:

5. Peep hole or alarm:

<u>Interior of home</u>

How many rooms?

Condition of home / cleanliness:

<u>Who has access?</u>

NAME	RELATION	PURPOSE	KEY? CODE? *

* Do they currently possess a key to your locks or know a code to your alarm?

Safes:
    A.   Is the safe hidden from view?

    B.   Who knows about the safe?

    C.   What is the value of its contents?

Places of concealment:
    1.   Do you have any corners that are difficult to look around?

    2.   Do you have any interior doors that remain shut most of the time?

    3.   In what part of the home do you spend the most amount of time?

    4.   How much of the inside of your home is exposed to your view from this location?

    5.   Are their any areas of the home that do not have an alternative escape route   (windowless room)?

Lighting:

LOCATION	TYPE	CONDITION	ILLUMINATION*

*How well is the room illuminated?

Electrical accessibility:

A.   Is the breaker box easily accessible?

B.   Are there any light switches that are not next to the doorway (Do you have to walk into a room in order to turn on the light)?

Phone accessibility:

1.   How many phones do you have?

2.   Are they easily accessible?

Weapons / self defense:

WEAPON TYPE	SECURE/ LOCKED	ACCESSIBLE	TRAINED*

*Have you received training for this device?

Valuable property/ money / visible / contained:

OBJECT	VISIBLE	ACCESSIBILITY	VALUE	ACKNOWLEDGED*

* Who knows about this item?

RISK ASSESSMENT EXAMPLE

This is a basic example of how to fill out a risk assessment survey. The answers used within this example are not real.

RISK ASSESSMENT SURVEY

1. Personal Information

Name: John Doe

Address: 534 Cherry Ln.

Number of occupants: 3

Occupations: Welder

Animals / Types: 2 dogs- black labs

Amount of Time Present: 14/24 hrs. of the day

Hours unoccupied: 8a.m. to 3 p.m.

2. Perimeter

Roads connected to property (how, how many): 1

Amount of traffic: moderate or low

Location within city / neighborhood: Older part of town. Neighborhood is run down in some areas.

Perimeter entrances/ how many, accessibility:

ENTRANCE	LOCKS	NECESSITY	ACCESSIBLE	CONCERN
Driveway	None	High	Easy	Open to sidewalk
Back Gate	Pad	Low	Fair	Neighbors kids

Condition of yard: The yard is in good condition and looks like it is well kept.

Fence / type / condition:

FENCE TYPE	CONDITION	PLACES/ NEED OF IMPROVEMENT
Wood	Fair	North side needs repairs

Gates / locks / who has access:

LOCATION	LOCKS	NECESSITY	ACCESSABLE/WHO?	CONCERN
South side	None	yes	Easy/ Joe, Cindy	Unsecured

Neighbors (Who, how many, problems, level of trust, history, interaction):

NAMES/ LOCATION	*TRUST	HISTORY, INTERACTION, CONCERNS
Bob, Jane Jones/ North	9	Known for a long time. No problems
Fred, Sarah Pack/ South	4	Problems in the past. Litters my yard. Has been arrested for drugs.
Henry Wilson/ Across	8	Widower, elderly, yard poorly kept.

*Level of Trust – 1-10 One being extremely untrustworthy, ten begin fully trustworthy

Garage/ shed (Condition):

Contents within outside structure (flammable liquids, tools, ATV):

OBJECT	VALUE	ACKNOWLEDGED, (WHO KNOW'S)
Lawn Mower	$300.00	Neighbors and family
4-wheeeler	$4500.00	Neighbors, family, coworkers
Tool chest	$250.00	Family, Jeff, Will and Jenny

Exterior lighting (YES OR NO):
   A.   Is the yard completely illuminated? **no**
   B.   Are the exterior walls of the home completely illuminated?
yes
   C.   Are the lights in full operation? **yes**
   D.   Are the lights easily accessible? **yes**
   E.   Are the lights easy to operate? **yes**
   F.   Are the lights controlled from inside? **yes**
   G.   Is there a battery backup for these lights? **no**

If you have answered NO to any of these questions, please explain:
The west corner of the back yard is dark, especially around the garage.
There is no battery back up for the outside lights. They are hooked up to the house.

Motion sensors / security system: driveway lights

    A.   Type and brand of sensor/ alarm: Acme Lights

    B.   Objective of the sensor/alarm (what does it do / cover?):
Illuminates when   triggered.

    C.   How does it operate? dependable

    D.   Performance history: It has worked well but is sensitive at times.

Mail box (condition, type, locking, vandalized): Good condition/ no vandalism

Vehicles/ amount / movement:

TYPE	CONDITION	VALUE	MOVEMENT
Toy. P/U	good	$6500	Frequent during the day

Have you ever caught someone in your yard before who did not have permission?
Once I scared away a transient who had wandered into my front yard. I have never seen him again.

3. Underline: Exterior of home

Color: **white**

General shape / design of home: **single level home**

Wall and structure material: **Brick, stucco**

Condition: **good**

Windows (Exterior and Interior inspection)

LOCATION	CONDITION	LOCK/ ALARM	HEIGHT*	EXPOSURE
front	good	One lock	4 ft.	lots
front	Broken lock	One lock	4 ft.	lots
South side	good	One lock	6 ft.	little
back	fair	One lock	4 ft.	little
back	poor	none	4 ft.	little

* Height from the ground

Height and condition of roof (Are there any low accessible places?):
Tin roof, good condition.

Entry Ways & Doors

ENTRY WAY #1
A.   Is the entry way or porch clean? **yes**
B.   Is the entire entry visible from inside the home? **yes**
C.   Is the entry way well lit? **yes**
D.   Does the entry way have steps? **yes**
E.   Are there additional doors besides the door to the house?
no
F.   Is the entry way enclosed? If so, can it be locked? **no**

Door
1.   Condition: **Wood door, no cracks or damage**

2.   Strength: **good**
3.   Usage: **frequent**

4.   Locks: **dead bolt**

5.   Peep hole or alarm: **no**

ENTRY WAY #2
A.   Is the entry way or porch clean? **yes**
B.   Is the entire entry way visible from inside the home? **yes**
C.   Is the entry way well lit? **yes**
D.   Does the entry way have steps? **no**
E.   Are there additional doors besides the door to the house? **yes**
F.   Is the entry way enclosed? If so, Can it be locked? **Yes, yes**

Door
1. Condition: **Wood door, no cracks or damage**

2. Strength: **good**

3. Usage: **seldom**

4. Locks: **door knob lock**

5. Peep hole or alarm: **no**

Interior of home

How many rooms? **9**

Condition of home / cleanliness: **well kept, clean**

Who has access?

NAME	RELATION	PURPOSE	KEY? CODE? *
Jane Doe	spouse	resident	house key
Janet Doe	Daughter	resident	house key
Frank James	Friend	house watch during vacation	house key
Martha Brown	Neighbor	key holder	house key

* Do they currently possess a key to your locks or know a code to your alarm?

Safes:
    A.   Is the safe hidden from view? **yes**

    B.   Who knows about the safe? **spouse**

    C.   What is the value of its contents? **$25,000.00**

Places of concealment:
    1.   Do you have any corners that are difficult to look around? **A sharp turn in the stairway to the basement.**

    2.   Do you have any interior doors that remain shut most of the time? **Storage room in the basement.**

3. What part of the home do you spend the most amount of time?
Family room

4. How much of the inside of your home is exposed to your view from this location? **Most of the   upstairs accept for part of the kitchen and   part of the   south bedrooms.**

5. Are their any areas of the home that do not have an alternative escape route   (windowless room)? **No**

Lighting:

LOCATION	TYPE	CONDITION	ILLUMINATION*
Front room	Hanging fix.	Good/ working	good
SE bed room	Lamp light	fair	dim
bathroom	Ceiling light	good	bright
kitchen	Ceiling light	good	dim

*How well is the room illuminated?

Electrical accessibility:
A. Is the breaker box easily accessible? **Yes, closet**
B. Are there any light switches that are not next to the   doorway (Do you have to walk into a room in order to turn on the light)? **Yes. SW bedroom**

Phone accessibility:
1. How many phones do you have? **2**
2. Are they easily accessible? **yes**

Weapons / self defense:

WEAPON TYPE	SECURE/ LOCKED	ACCESSIBLE	TRAINED*
.357	yes	yes	yes
shotgun	yes	no	yes
taser	no	yes	no

*Have you received training for this device?

Valuable property/ money / visible / contained:

OBJECT	VISABLE	ACCESSIBILITY	VALUE	ACKNOWLEDGED*
Painting	yes	yes	$1200	Family, Frank, June
Cash	no	no	$15,000	Family
TV	yes	yes	$1,000	Family, Frank, Bob
stereo	yes	no	$850.00	Family, Frank, Bob

* Who knows about this item?

SECURING THE PERIMETER
Chapter 3

SECURING THE PERIMETER
Chapter 3

Many homeowners enjoy the privacy of a fenced in yard. A solid fence can serve many purposes such as secluding and securing valuable property, keep children and animals out of the street and provide privacy from those who pass by on the sidewalk or street. A fence is always a good investment when working to secure your home and property.

There are several types of fences on the market today ranging in price, quality and stability. For those who can afford one, a cinderblock or cement wall can definitely provide the seclusion a homeowner might wish to have. However, even though these types of wall are certainly the strongest available, that does not necessarily mean they are the most secure.

Choosing the right fence is important and when choosing a fence the final decision will always depend on two factors; need and price.

Need

Before buying a fence, consider what type of security you are looking for. Consider what you are trying to secure and decide what type of a fence will best strengthen your perimeter. For example, if you have a number of automobiles, ATV's or prize winning animals in your back yard, you want a fence that will not only keep thieves out but will also keep your items in. Stringing a simple wire fence around your property will not provide the security you need. A thief would have little trouble cutting the wires and pulling back the fence to provide an exit with your valuable property. If the items you are securing are large like a car or an ATV, consider installing a fence that is more difficult to remove. If the money is available, cinderblock or cement walls provide excellent coverage, minimizing your weak points to the gate.

When cinderblock or cement is not an option, consider putting in a large chain link fence constructed of at least nine gauge wire. Make sure that the poles are spread to only about five feet apart preventing a vehicle from passing through. Also, be sure that the fence is at least six feet tall. Combined with a secure gate, this fence will provide excellent security.

Barbwire is an effective way to keep an intruder from scaling a fence. But barbwire is also an unattractive addition to a yard and sometimes even prohibited in certain residential areas. Barbwire or razor wire is best used for perimeter control around home based businesses that are secluded or distanced from neighbors. When installed, the wire should extend outward from the top of the fence making it extremely difficult to climb over.

Wood Fence

A wood fence requires far more upkeep that metal or cement fences. However, when the posts are placed closer together, between three and five feet apart, a wood fence can become almost as effective as a chain link. A wood fence must be kept up. Annual inspections of a wood fence are vital to find and repair any damage or warped boards. Also, to increase the life of a wood fence, it is important to coat it with a waterproofing sealer or paint. This will allow the fence to withstand the elements as well as ad beauty to the yard.

Price
The price of a good fence can vary dramatically between different types. A cement or block wall will be far more expensive that a wood or chain link and is often times not as effective. Even though they are a much more solid fence they are easier to scale than a wood or chain link.

When picking out a good fence strongly consider what your price range is and what you can afford without going into too much debt. Often times you find that the most important purpose of fences are simply to establish your perimeter. Once you have done that there are other, less expensive methods for increasing security such as motion sensors and even barb wire.

A popular alternative to wood, block, cement or steel is vinyl. Vinyl fences have become a top choice because of their attractive appearance and low hassle. However, vinyl can wear and crack over time from long exposure to sunlight. Also, once a piece of vinyl fencing has been damaged or broken, it can be difficult to replace or repair that section. Vinyl fences do help to beautify a yard, and many types and designs do provide excellent concealment, but their long term problems should not be overlooked when considering this type of fence.

Gates

A gate is often looked upon as the weakest point on a fence. However, that is often far from the truth. A gate is secured with a lock and is usually located in an exposed area. Most intruders will avoid the gate and take their chances with other areas of the fence.

Even though the main body of the fence is more subject to intruders, it is vital to secure every gate with a lock. The gate, much like the door to your home is the entrance and exit to your property. If a gate is left unsecured, anybody can simply walk in before you have a chance to react.

Common latch for residential use.

The latch that you select for your fence should be sturdy enough to withstand a kick or push from the opposite side. Examine the latch to see how well the two components connect when the gate is closed. If there is a lot of play in the system, you might want to consider replacing the latch assembly.

Padlocks are a good way to secure a gate from the inside. An intruder has limited access to the lock and therefore will make little attempt at picking it. If your gate is locked from the outside, a padlock can also be used but will not provide the same level of security. Any time a lock is exposed to an intruder, it becomes more vulnerable to pound open or pick. The best solution to securing the gate from the outside is to either have an electronic key combination lock or a combination box over the padlock.

Padlocks are a good way to secure a gate

One important aspect to keeping a gate secure is to know who has access. Combination locks or key padlocks should only be accessible by those who have your permission. If you lend a key to your lock out to someone who may be taking care of your yard or pet, be sure to get the key back after the favor has been completed. If possible, have the keys stamped with the words DO NOT COPY or NO COPY to help insure that additional copies are not produced.

When using a key pad lock, only have as many keys as necessary. For example, If three people in your family each need a key then make only 4 and secure one as a spare. Be sure to lock up the spare in a secure location. If one of the keys is stolen or lost, replace the entire pad lock instead of paying a locksmith to re key it. With pad locks only costing a few dollars, this will save you a huge expense.

Another option is to attach a combination key holder on or around the lock. This secure box will hold your key at the gate, eliminating the hassle of having to carry and keep track of other copies. You simply dial in the combination and the box opens to allow access to your key.

Combination locks, depending on make and model can be changed as necessary. If you are using a combination lock which has a fixed combination, meaning you cannot change it yourself; simply buy a new one whenever necessary. However, if the combination can be changed it will usually come with a small bar or key needed to unlock the current combination. Remember to keep that bar when you first open the package as you will need it later on to change the combination.

In conclusion, a wood fence is probably the most effective way to secure a residential perimeter without paying too much money. As long as a wooden fence is well kept, it will provide the necessary security that a yard needs. To increase that security, be sure that the fence is built with all the posts and framework located on the inside of the yard. The framework of a wooden fence can serve as a ladder for unwanted intruders. Many wood fences are built so that the posts are staggered or exposed on both sides. This allows neighbors to have both the solid and framework appearance. Though attractive in appearance, this design will decrease the security of the fence. When possible, keep all frameworks on the inside (your side of the fence).

SECURING YOUR YARD
Chapter 4

SECURING YOUR YARD
Chapter 4

Securing your property can be a simple and inexpensive task. Too often, homeowners will sink into debt and build a large wall between them and their neighbors. When done right, this can be an attractive addition to a yard, but often times can also turn a yard into a prison. Beauty does not have to be sacrificed for security.

Front Yard

Many homeowners prefer to not have a fence around their front yard. In neighborhoods where neighbors are also good friends, people want their home to look inviting and without restriction. When this is the case, there are limited methods for security during daylight hours that can be used to keep unwanted intruders off your property. One method would be a motion sensor that will set off a signal within your home, warning you of someone approaching.

After dark, security becomes easier for an open front yard. Exterior lighting that illuminates both the yard and home will often scare away many home invaders.

Exterior Lighting   Motion Activated

Exterior Lighting

Exterior lighting presents too much of a challenge for a burglar. Unless the thief has a specific object to steal or is completely intent on robbing or invading a specific home, he will more than likely move on to a target with less illumination. For most thieves, the easier the target, the better. A well illuminated home becomes difficult to sneak around especially in a neighborhood or on a busy street.

Exterior lighting is usually a standard item in new homes, and many older homes are wired to accommodate outside lighting. If a

homeowner does not have exterior lighting, it would be wise to have exterior lighting installed by a licensed electrician. However, if lighting installation is too expensive, there are alternatives for lighting, such as battery operated and solar charging lights. These are a good addition to have even if there is exterior lighting on a home or property, simply for the fact that electricity can fail leaving a house vulnerable to intrusion.

Motion activated driveway lights are another good method, and the solar powered models can be installed anywhere in the yard. Furthermore, they will not add to your electric bill because they are self sufficient.

The placement of exterior lights is just as important as having them in the first place. For most homes built within the last twenty years, exterior lighting is added into the construction and the homeowner has little influence as to where the lighting is placed. Often times, lights will be placed next to or above all entry ways and on the corners of the home, below the eves. The exterior lights located on the corners of the home should be a spot light model, or lights that can be rotated and pointed in several directions. This allows both sides of the corner to be well illuminated.

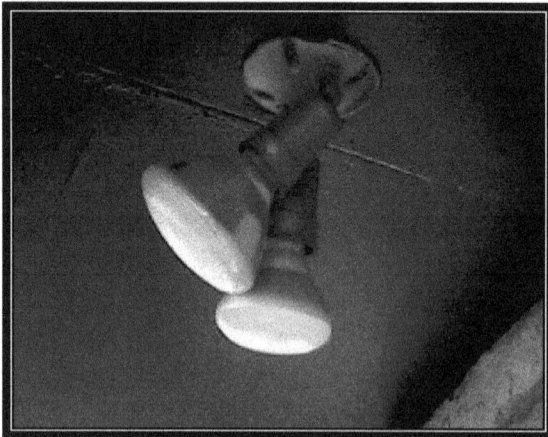

Spot Lights

Exterior lighting should shine down towards the walls of a house, pointing mostly to the base of the wall. This will illuminate the exterior of the house and create a three to eight foot area (depending on size and strength of lights) of exposure around the home.

Motion Alarms

Battery or solar charged motion alarms can be placed anywhere within the yard. Much like motion lights, the alarm system is triggered when someone or something passes through the sight of the sensor. A signal is sent to a monitoring device inside the home which sounds an alarm or chime, alerting of an intrusion. These systems are excellent for areas of the yard that may be hard to see from inside the home. Motion alarms are triggered by heat so they are effective night and day. Remember, when purchasing such items for yard security, be sure to buy only those types of systems that can handle harsh weather conditions.

Cameras

Cameras are becoming a more popular solution to crime prevention and apprehension, especially in commercial areas. As technology advances, owning security cameras is as common as an additional lock on a front door. In fact, the various wireless systems available today are not only easy to install and inexpensive to buy, but also the cut out the need to hire an electrician.

When installing security cameras in your yard the first thing you want to be sure of is to purchase OUTDOOR cameras. Interior camera models will burn out the first time they are exposed to moisture.

The next step to camera security would be to determine how many you need and where you will need them. Through careful planning, you can eliminate the additional expense to buying extra cameras you don't really need. For example, if your front yard is between 60 and 100 feet wide, one camera placed on a top corner of your house should provide all the visual coverage that you need. However, if you have several concealed locations (discussed later in this chapter) then more cameras might be necessary for complete coverage. Once the number of cameras and their locations are determined, the next step would be finding an adequate location for both the transmitter device and the monitor. Some models are designed to install into your television for added convenience. For example, suppose you are watching television and you hear something outside.

With a click of a button your screen will change to the view from the cameras so that you can see what is in your yard.

Night vision cameras are a must for a home or business. This feature will certainly add to the cost but without it, your cameras are useless after nightfall. There are some exceptions when a regular camera will pick up visibility under extreme exterior illumination. However, your exterior lighting would have to be incredibly bright to compensate for the sunlight the camera requires for success.

Vegetation

If a homeowner wants a small picket fence in the front yard or no fence at all, but still wishes to somehow separate their yard from the street and sidewalk, certain plants and bushes can create a secure perimeter. Planting a thick hedge can create an almost impassible barrier between a yard and sidewalk. The height and width of the hedge should help to determine each other for the maximum amount of security. For example, if you wish to have a hedge behind you four foot picket fence but do not wish it to be any taller than the fence posts, the hedge should therefore be wider, nothing less than three feet thick. In contrast, if you wish to have a tall hedge then thicker is always better but not as necessary as a shorter cut.

Hedge

Using vegetation for security in your yard can be effective, but does require upkeep. Always maintain your hedges and bushes, keeping them healthy and well trimmed. A clean yard will show a responsible homeowner, one that will defend his home if invaded.

Another effective way to use vegetation and plants for security is to place thorny bushes and plants below the windows of your home. In warm, desert climates, cacti are a beautiful addition to a yard, especially when they bloom. However, they are also an intruder's worst nightmare when trying to gain entry through a window located behind the plant. Rose bushes are much the same especially when they have grown 3 to 5 feet in height. Any attempts to push down, trample or remove these plants will usually cause enough noise and alert you that someone is outside.

Dogs

Dogs can serve as both a warning and protector

Dogs can be a great warning device when an unknown person approaches a yard or home. Regardless of size, dogs are a very territorial animal and when they feel threatened, they take instinctive action, usually barking, to stop a possible threat. But, as any dog owner will tell you, owning a dog is far different than simply owning a security system. Dogs require feeding, water, love, attention and plenty of space to run and play. A dog is a living, breathing creature that will instinctively adopt you as its family if you give them what it needs for a good healthy life.

There have been several cases where a female dog becomes protective of their owners children. This can be a great advantage when children are playing in the yard; a dog will not only play with the children but will fend off possible kidnappers. Like people, each dog is different, some are protective and others are not. When shopping for a family dog that will also provide security, consult a veterinarian, dog trainer, or pet store owner to see which dog is best for you. If you have children, be sure to select a dog that is child friendly whose tolerance level is high. Children can be rough with a dog sometimes as well as noisy and hyper. These actions can frustrate some dogs and even cause

them to become defensive. In addition to finding a patient, loving dog, your children should learn how to respect and care for your dog so that a friendship will develop.

Be sure to examine your lifestyle to determine if you need a dog. Dogs need time and space to run and play. They also require attention and love regardless of how strenuous your schedule may be. By spending adequate time with your dog, they will become more loyal and devoted to you, their master. You can also use this time to teach and train your dog so that they will not bark, scare or attack innocent bystanders, or people who come to your door. All it takes is one bite on the wrong person, and your dog will be put to sleep. Time and training are essential!

<u>Places of Concealment</u>

As mythical as movies and television shows can be, one thing stands to be true- bad guys do lurk in the shadows. Although many intruders today use the smash and grab or smash and surprise methods of invading a home, most intruders still try to stay concealed and undetected when committing their crime. To prevent these types of criminals from invading your home, eliminate the "shadows" throughout your yard.

The best method for finding these concealed places is to first stand on your front or back porch and examine your yard in its entirety. Are there places that you cannot see from where you are standing? Are their corners big enough to conceal a man from view? Are there objects in the yard or vehicles parked that could serve as a hiding place for an intruder?

Small walkway between a garage and trees.

When observing from the front porch, consider your path to the mail box, street, driveway, or even a garbage can. Are their places between the house and those objectives where a grown man could hide in wait to attack you? Thinking defensively will help you to pinpoint areas of concern. If possible, remove these places or objects of concealment. If removal is not an option increase the lighting around these locations to eliminate all darkness. Regardless of how concealed they are, lighting always makes criminals nervous and doubtful about their plan of attack. In extreme cases, mirrors can even be installed to help you see around corners before approaching them.

Another method to consider when finding places of concealment is to think like an intruder. For a moment, go on the offense and begin from the end of your yard and make your way to the house. When attempting to stay concealed, where does your instinct first tell you to go? Once you are there, where is you next point of concealment?

By doing this, you can see from the criminals perspective, how, why and where your home and property are vulnerable targets. If possible, have someone stand on your porch and watch as you try to conceal yourself in different places. If they cannot see you, you have a place of concealment that an intruder will definitely pick up on.

Conclusion

Exterior lighting is an important aspect to securing your home. A well lit home will often be passed by when intruders are looking for a victim. Exterior lighting should shine towards the base of the exterior walls to create a area of exposure around the home.

Motion alarms and cameras are useful in securing your home. Motion alarms will trigger an alarm within the home when someone or something passes in front of the sensor. Cameras, unless constantly or frequently monitored will not warn of an invasion into the yard but rather will capture a visual of the intruder for later apprehension or evidence. Motion alarms and cameras can also serve as effective warning devices for concealed areas within the yard. Before approaching these hard to see areas, a motion alarm or camera monitor can be checked to ensure that all is well before proceeding.

Vegetation such as roses, cactus and thorn bushes can serve as additional security when planted beneath vulnerable windows. Using vegetation for additional security will also add beauty to your yard and home.

Dogs are an effective way to keeping unwanted intruders out of your yard and home. However, dogs require the basics needs as we humans do such as food, water shelter, attention and love. They also need room and time to play and exercise. Owning a dog can be a wonderful thing but only if a dog can properly fit into your life and schedule.

Places of concealment are best overcome when they are detected early. If a grown adult can hide behind a wall or object within the yard, that becomes a place of concern. Lighting mirrors and rearranging can help to overcome these vulnerable areas.

DOORS AND WINDOWS
Chapter 5

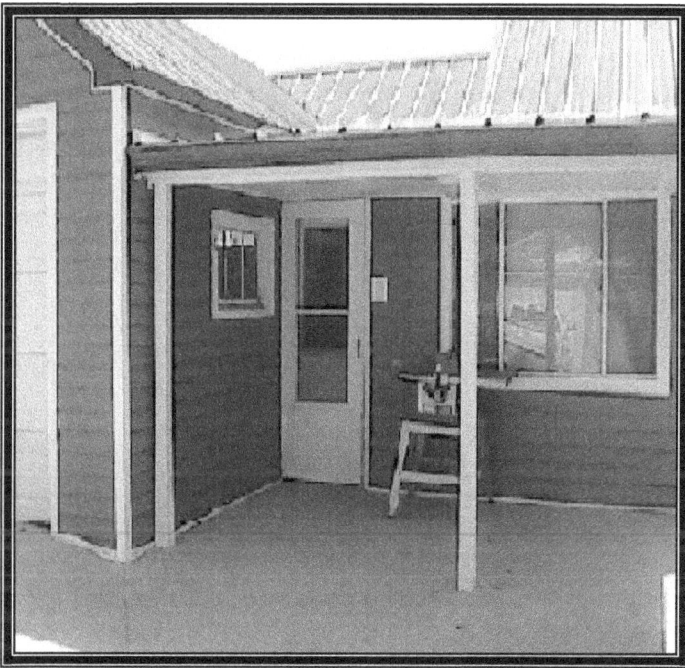

DOOR AND WINDOWS
Chapter 5

It is with little doubt that the most vulnerable areas of your home are its doors and windows. Much like a traditional castle with tall, thick block walls circled about by a deep and swampy moat, the gate is where many invaders often placed their focus of attack simply because any attempt on the wall would be useless.

For most houses, the exterior sides of its walls are protected by brick or stone. Though they are not bulletproof and have been brought down before by criminals using a car or sledge hammer, walls are generally left alone by intruders who focus more on doors and windows.

There are hundreds of models of doors and windows on the market today varying in shape, size and color. Securing a door or window, regardless of its shape and size, is generally done with the same basic methods. However, the quality of a door and window can also vary and these can play important factors in how you secure these areas.

Doors

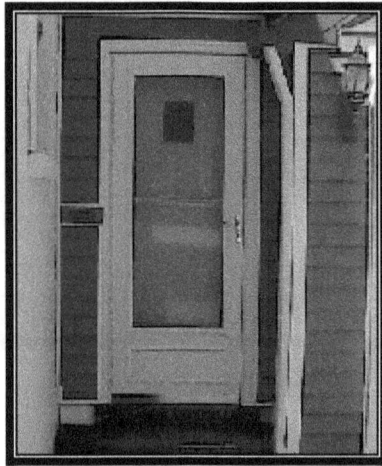

Wood door with locking screen door

The attractiveness of a door has become more important than ever as people attempt to create a beautiful entry way. Solid wood doors help to give a home that elaborate, yet rustic appearance, while a steel door modernizes a home. Either way, be sure that the door is solid and able to withstand extreme force or pressure from outside.

As previously mentioned in this book, your weakest area of a door is the link between the door and the frame. In this area, the latch from the door knob and dead bolt (if applicable) stick out from the opening edge of the door and into a hole in the frame. When the door knob or dead bolt is turned, the latch is pulled back into the door, freeing it from the frame and wall.

Door Knob and Dead Bolt

As common as these locks and latches are, no matter how advanced they may seem, or how strong the steel bolts and latches may appear, they are only as strong as the door and frame which hold them. For example, if a door is shut and locked, the latch will not retract and therefore stay sticking inside the door frame. However, if the frame around the latch is weak, a strong force from the outside of the door can cause the frame around the latch to break allowing the door to fly open. Kicking and slamming a front door open is becoming a popular method for forced entry attacks. By breaking the door down, the intruder can take the homeowner by surprise and stop them from reacting or running for help. A knowledgeable intruder will know if a door can be kicked down, simply by observing its strength, and what it is constructed of.

A battered door frame that needs to be replaced

There are several ways to reinforce a door frame to add strength around the latch such as drilling 3" wood screws on the inside of the frame to increase its strength.

A door frame temporarily secured with 4" screws

However, the best method of defense would be to replace the old frame with a new steel one. If this is too expensive then, try to reinforce the frame with sheet metal or additional wood screws that will help to keep the frame intact in case the door is slammed or kicked from the outside.

By learning about the many different locks available and by deciding just how much security you really need you will save money by buying only what you need. For doors of all types there are at least two locks that are highly recommended. The first is a key driven lock systems such as a dead bolt or those found in most exterior door assemblies. Though picking these locks can be quite easy for a professional to do, they do keep out the common intruder who is acting on instinct and doesn't know about picking locks. Furthermore, these locks allow you to secure your home from the outside by using a key.

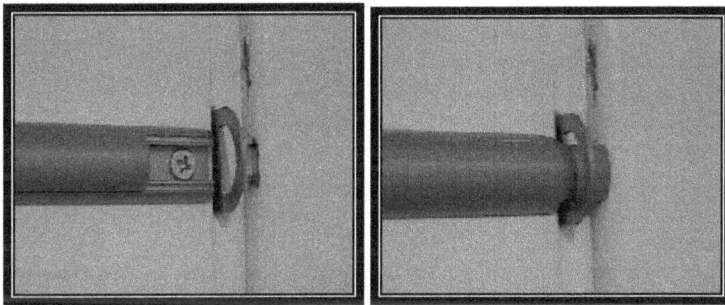

Simple slide latch system

The second type of lock is a latch system that can only be operated from the inside. There are many models on the market to choose from and some are stronger than others. For example, the simple sliding latch system as show in the picture is probably the most secure latch system on the market. Interestingly enough, it is also one of the least expensive.

Other latch systems include levers which flip from the door frame over a ball joint which is connected to the door. This is a somewhat effective latch but due to its design, it has a weak spot on both ends where the latch and joint are connected to the door and frame.

Latch lock

You may have also seen a chain lock which acts similar to a latch sliding over to the frame. These chain locks are good for opening the door enough to see the other side but without having to give up your security. The down side to chain locks is that the chain is the main weakness for the assembly and will often times break off where it is mounted to the wall.

Door alarms are another inexpensive and highly effective alert system that every door should have. A common magnetic alarm device can cost anywhere from $4.00 to $50.00 depending on your price range. Simple in design, these alarms come in two pieces, one attaching to the door and the other to the frame. The pieces fit close together when the door is shut. When the alarm is turned on there is a magnetic connection between the two parts of the alarm. When the door is opened the magnetic connection is broken, setting off the alarm siren.

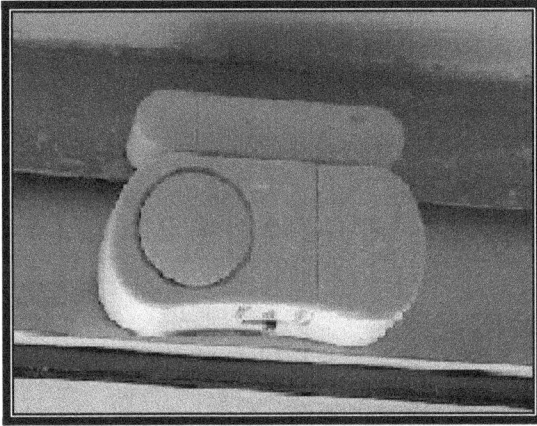
Bunker Hill door and window alarm

Many times when an intruder sets an alarm off and the ear piercing siren is blazing through the house, they will flee the scene to avoid getting caught, thus making the alarm a deterrent. However, the main function of the alarm is alert you when a door or window has been open. These alarms are especially useful during the day if you have a young child who learns how to open doors and windows. If the alarm is positioned up high, the child cannot turn it off and therefore is unable to open the door or window undetected.

Windows

Exterior Windows

The most efficient homes on the market today are those with large, sturdy windows. Windows are essential for light, fresh air, and cooling. But windows can also be an inviting entryway for unwanted intruders.

Windows that are ten years or older are often installed with a metal or wood frame. Though good at the time of installation, these types of windows are now a burglars dream come true. Old wooden or metal frames can easily be manipulated with a screw driver or crow bar. Most of these windows were also assembled with a locking system that can now be easily unlatched. For example, suppose you have a 2 piece window and the bottom pane opens by sliding up. In the center of this window, where the two frames join when the window is closed there is a half circle latch which rotates around and engages a port or hole to lock the window. Because the window is wood or metal older than 10 years, an experienced burglar can slide a screw driver, saw blade, clothes hanger or some kind of rod up between the two joining frames and apply pressure to the latch causing it to release from the port.

Windows that open from the bottom

If you have windows that may be questionable in regards to security, there are a few simple tests you can try to determine how vulnerable they really are. First, take both hands and apply pressure directly to the outside of a sliding window (the part of the window that opens). WARNING: DO NOT APPLY EXTREME PRESSURE THAT WILL CAUSE THE GLASS TO BREAK AND SHATTER!! Simply apply gentle pressure and observe around the frame of the window. If the joining frames (as described in the example above) separate more than a 2 mm, your window can be picked. Remember, foam, sealer or weather stripping will not stop an object from coming through the space between your frames.

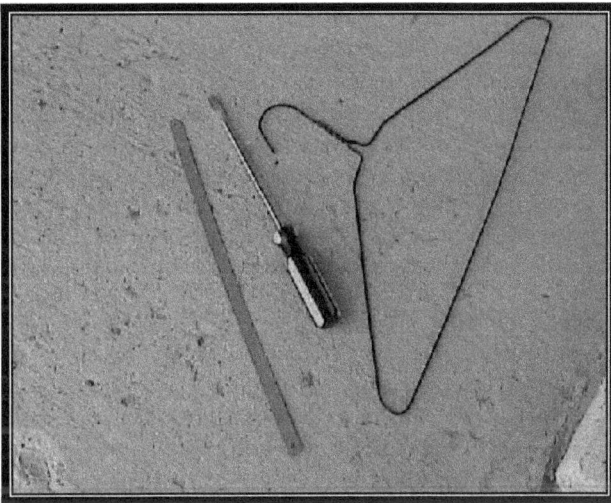

Saw blades, screwdrivers, and clothes hangers can be used to open windows

Window alarms are similar to doors alarms that consist of two parts connected by a magnetic hold. When the magnetic hold is broken, the alarm will sound until the magnetic hold is reconnected or the alarm is turned off. These are highly effective and inexpensive. These types of alarms are good for windows that are seldom opened. Depending on the model, battery life should last from six months to one year.

Another type of window alarm is the vibration alarm which, unlike the door/window alarm that attaches to the framework, attaches directly to the glass. Its purpose is to detect any movement in the window pane such as pressing, cutting or braking. Once vibration is detected, the alarm is triggered and can only be shut off with the switch on the alarm. These alarms can be used on both opening and non opening windows.

Blinds are an important purchase when increasing the security of your windows. Blinds will not conceal most indoor lighting but will prevent an intruder from knowing who or what is inside the home. During the day or at night when the lights are off in the house, blinds can be left open and visibility from outside is still limited. When the sun goes down and the interior lights go on, the inside of a home can be as visible as a movie screen. By closing blinds, an intruder is limited on knowledge and therefore may hesitate to break in. Most blinds are simply a deterrent for crime and not necessarily a stopping tool. However, blinds can be noisy when bumped up against and will certainly make noise when someone is entering through the window. To help prevent against an intruder from reaching in and pulling the lanyard to raise the blinds, simply roll up the cord and hook it on the wall above the blinds (this is also a good idea when little children are present and the lanyard is a choke or hanging hazard). If an intruder has opened the window and popped out the screen he will next reach for the lanyard to quietly lift the blinds. If he cannot find the cord he will either make a lot of noise searching for it or will attempt to enter the home around the blinds and make a lot of noise in the process.

Conclusion

Doors and windows are the most vulnerable spots on a home because they open and close and are usually secured with a single latch or bolt. The strength and stability of a door is just as important as the lock or knob assembly. An exterior door should be constructed of solid wood or steel with a locking door knob and an interior latching system.
Window locks can be easily manipulated with simple items such as clothes hangers, saw blades and screw drivers. The best method for securing windows is to first replace old window frames with new vinyl models that have a newer latching lock. The next best method for securing locks would be to install window or vibration alarms that are triggered when the window is opened, cut or broken.

INTERIOR
PROTECTION
Chapter 6

INTERIOR PROTECTION
Chapter 6

Feeling safe and secure in your own home depends on several factors such as, how well do you know the layout of your house or who has access into your home? Questions such as these can be answered and resolved by conducting the risk assessment in chapter two as well as walking through the home and examining each room from different angles.

Blind Spots

Every home has blind spots throughout it, even small, open studio apartments. A blind spot is any location throughout the home where an intruder can conceal themselves from your view. This may sound like a simple hiding place but the difference between a blind spot and a hiding place is a blind spot is used during movement throughout the home rather than being a fixed location. For example, if you are sitting in your front room and directly off the south of the room is a hallway which leads to an office or bedroom. From where you are sitting you are unable to see into the hallway beyond two feet. Therefore, the hallway is a blind spot in which an intruder can stand out of your line of sight.

Blind spot entering a bedroom

Blind spots are a rapists best weapon! They are usually located in a lane of travel which provides a great opportunity to take someone by surprise. Consider the example above- a young lady who is sitting in her front room is completely unaware that a man has broken in through a window in the back bedroom. The intruder, after entering the home, makes his way to the blind spot in the hallway and purposely begins to make a little noise. The young lady, hearing the noise, gets up to investigate and is taken by surprise in the hallway.

The best way to expose these types of areas throughout your home is to either move your furniture in such a way as to see all of your surroundings, or purchase a decorative mirror and hang it on the wall so that it will show you around hard to see corners. Using the example above, suppose the young lady had a mirror hanging on the wall so that from where she was sitting could see into the hallways blind spot. She would have noticed the intruder and escaped through a different exit. Remember, mirrors are a great way to reveal blind spots but they can also be used by the intruder to look at you. In vulnerable situations such as, being home alone, having received a previous threat or hearing suspicious noises, make it a point to glance a the mirror every one to three minutes. It is better that you notice them before they see you.

Blind Spot around a corner

Much like a yard, the number of blind spots within a home depends largely upon the design of the home and the amount of furniture it has. Also like a yard, cleanliness is key to having the upper hand. When your home is in order you know where everything is or where it should be. A clean, well organized home will reduce the number of blind spots. You will then be more in tuned with the spots that you cannot prevent because of the layout of the home.

Motion Alarms

Motion alarms can be a wonderful source of security, both in and out of the home. Their simple design can be easy to operate and install. The basic concept behind these types of alarms is simply to notify you that someone or something is moving in designated area covered by the sensor on the alarm. As with all alarm systems, the make, model and cost can very significantly. But high prices do not always mean better product, so be wise when shopping for motion alarms.

When using a motion alarm, consider the following questions:
1. What am I trying to protect?
2. How far do I need the sensor to reach?
3. How much of a warning do I want?
4. Do I need electrical power or battery power for best performance?

Some motion alarms can plug into a regular wall outlet and will detect any movement within a room. These simple models are good for concealment and will often be designed with an outlet in itself so that it does not entirely occupy the wall outlet.

A battery operated motion alarm has a broader range of use because it is not fixed to an outlet or wire. These alarms will often come in two pieces, the sensor and the monitor. When setting up a battery operated motion alarm, you first set the sensor pointing in the direction you wish to secure and turn it on. You then keep the monitor with you so that you can hear the alarm in the event that the sensor detects motion. If the sensor detects motion, it will trigger an alarm, either within itself or send the alert to your monitor which will then sound an alarm.

Deciding on the best make or model depends on your situation. For most people and homes, a battery operated motion alarm is recommended for it easy placement and independence from a fix power source. Also, a battery operated alarm can be taken on trips, to work or any new location where additional security is desired.

Vibration Alarms

When securing a house, it becomes obvious that the most vulnerable areas of the structure are the doors and windows. However, when securing an apartment or duplex, the situation changes because you share a wall, roof or ceiling with someone else. Though hard to believe, these shared surfaces can mean easy access into your home.

Though it usually happens to businesses, breaking through a wall of an apartment can and does happen. Found especially in cheap apartment complexes, the walls which divide each apartment can be poorly constructed and have little insulation. These walls are nothing more than sheet rocks, insulation and wood framing. More expensive apartment buildings have thicker, more secure walls to keep out noise and regulate varying temperatures between each apartment.

Breaking through a wall to rob an apartment is unwise for more than just the obvious reasons. Just because the wall is easy to break through, doesn't mean the cover up will be the same. When a renter returns to their apartment and finds a large hole in the wall that leads to their neighbor's apartment, it takes little evidence to show that the neighbor had something to do with it or knows who did.

To secure any walls, floors or ceilings that are shared with a neighbor, place vibration alarms in central locations across the vulnerable surface. Much like a window alarm, a vibration alarm is relatively small and has a simple ON an OFF switch on the side. But unlike the window alarm, the vibration alarm is activated by movement of the surface to which it is attached instead of a magnetic disconnection.

VIBRATION ALARM

Depending on the quality of alarm, two alarms should be necessary for a wall 25' in length. If someone tries to cut through the sheetrock, the vibrations from the saw will trigger the alarm and warn anyone nearby. Often times the alarm will cause the intruder to panic and quit his attempt to break through.

Self Defense

So far, this book has taught you methods for preventing, deterring or warning of unwanted intruders. But what happens when all these steps fail to keep someone out of your home? Remember, as mentioned in the beginning of the book, NO SYSTEM IS BULLETPROOF.

Most of the time, alarms, locks and other preventive devices will keep you safe from intruders. Using these devices can help prevent dangerous encounters with kidnappers, thieves, and rapists. But despite the effort put in to securing a home or property, some systems fail to keep intruders out. Because of these cases, it is best to have a self defense plan available and ready.

There are many things you can do to help insure your safety within your own home. First, always have quick access to a phone. If you hear or see someone breaking into your home, a call to the police will ensure your survival during a possible attack. Be sure to find out which method of contact is preferred in your town or city. Most locations use the simple 911 phone number for reporting emergencies. Regardless of what the number may be, program the police contact number into the speed dial system of your phone.

Another good method to consider is to always have a plan of escape. Never spend too long in a room that has only one exit. An exit can consist of a door or window that will allow you to remove yourself from the home or to a safe location where you can receive assistance. Some secondary exits may lead you onto the roof or balcony which should only be done if the escape is safe. Once you are on the roof or balcony, yell for help and try to get the attention of people down below.

Stun Gun

A stun gun is a device that can shoot a high voltage of electricity through a target, such as an attacker. These weapons come in two basic style, the first being a fixed prong style and the second, a prong shooting system or taser, as many are called. Both models are effective and have their place in self defense.

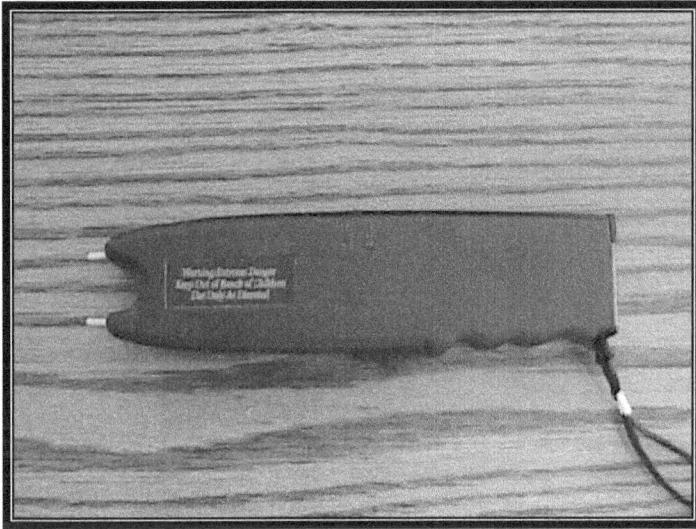

Stun Gun or Taser

The fixed prong style comes in various sizes ranging from 20 inches to 3 inches. Some models have even been disguised as cell phones or pens. The fixed prong style is used in a close contact situation. In order to shock an attacker, the victim must flip on a power switch, press the prongs against the attacker and then press another switch which fires the voltage. When practiced, this weapon can be effective against an attacker who surprises you from behind or grabs you in any way.

In order to strike the attacker, you must have enough movement with your arm or hand to activate the gun and press it somewhere on the attacker's body. In most cases, do not be picky about where you strike the attacker, hit them where you can and the electricity will take care of the rest.

The prong shooting taser has the same concept as the fixed prong models with the additional capability of firing the prongs at a distance. Many police departments use these models because it allows the officer to stop an attacker before he gets too close. Much like a gun, a taser is aimed at its target. When the target is within sight and range the operator pulls the trigger and fires two prongs at the target. The prongs stick to the target and begin delivering electricity. The amount of voltage that the target receives can be regulated by the operator, thus allowing the target to be detained for a period of time.

The downside to these models is the expensive cost for the air cartridges. Air cartridges are what propel the prongs towards the target. Each time the taser is fired, a new cartridge must be purchased.

Firearms

As previously mentioned in the book, firearms can be an effective method if self defense when handled correctly. Firearms should never be used to protect property or material possessions. Rather, a firearm should be used when your life or the life of another is directly threatened and there is no other alternative to prevent the attack.

Firearm training is an absolute must, even if you have been raised with and are familiar with guns. Firearm training will not only teach you about safety in possessing a firearm, but it will also teach how and when to use one.

Concealed weapon permits are another form of firearm safety. These permits allow an individual to carry a loaded concealed handgun in any public facility that is not previously restricted by the law such as government buildings and churches. If a concealed permit course is taught successfully, the students will learn the basics in handling a firearm and when to use one for self defense. The recommended calibers of handguns recommended for concealed carriers are 9mm, .38 Spec., .357, and .45.

The National Rifle Association (NRA) offers a wide variety of training courses in handling firearms. These classes are strongly recommended when considering buying a firearm for personal protection. They will also teach you about storing and maintaining your weapon.

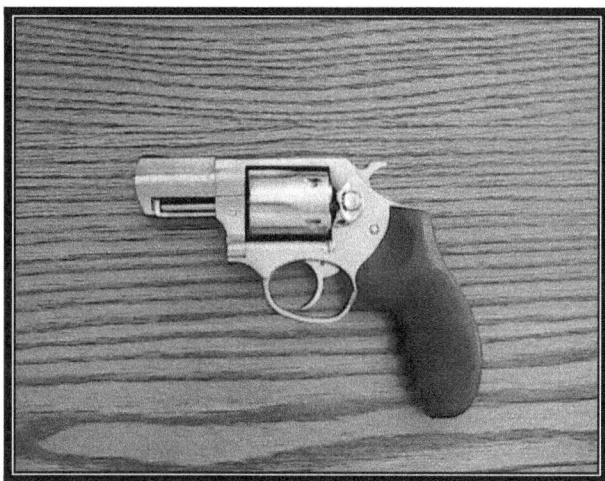
Ruger SP101 .357 Mag.

Remember, the gunslingers and shootouts you see in movies and on television are mostly fictional. Most situations involving a firearm for self defense end after one or two shots are fired and are immediately followed by a police investigation. If it is found that your actions were unjustified, not only will you lose your right to gun ownership but you will also certainly spend a significant time in prison, depending on the condition of the victim. Firearms can and will protect you when necessary, but sound judgment is crucial when using a gun for self defense.

NOTE: The instructions within this book do not qualify as firearm training but rather as a guide to getting prepared for gun ownership. Proper gun handling should be taught only from a licensed instructor.

Conclusion

Blind spots are a perfect hiding place for intruders. By walking through your home and viewing each room and hallway from different angles, you will become more aware of these vulnerable spots when approaching them. Also, you can use mirrors or rearrange your furniture to eliminate blind spots throughout your home.

Motion alarms and vibration alarms help to secure the inside of your home. Motion alarms are triggered when someone moves within the range of the sensor. Vibration Alarms are triggered by vibrations along the surface they are attached to.

Two methods of self defense are stun guns and firearms. Stun guns or tasers shoot electricity through an attacker when the prongs on the weapon make contact with the individual. Firearms are a last resort in self defense and should only be used against an immediate threat to your life or the life of another. Firearm training from a licensed profession is a must for proper gun ownership.

ABOUT THE AUTHOR

Keith Robison has been involved with security for several years. In 2003 he became a certified Locksmith and began researching new methods of home security.

While serving in the Utah Army National Guard, Keith served in various activations, the first being security duty during the 2002 Winter Olympics in Salt Lake City. He later went on to serve on a training activation in Ft. Lewis, Washington during Operation Enduring Freedom. He concluded his military service with a tour of duty in Iraq during Operation Iraqi Freedom.

He earned an Associates of Applied Science in Criminal Justice from Kaplan University in 2007 and currently resides in Utah with his wife and two children.

Keith Robison currently offers security consulting for residential and commercial locations. To contact Keith, email him at keithrobison97@hotmail.com.

www.ingramcontent.com/pod-product-compliance
Lightning Source LLC
LaVergne TN
LVHW091208080426
835509LV00006B/898